THE SCIENCE FAIR PROJECT
A Step-by-Step Guide

THE SCIENCE FAIR PROJECT
A-Step by-Step Guide

SECOND EDITION 2017

ISBN: 978-1482600346

Cover Design by Bradley & Paige Hudson

FOR MORE COPIES WRITE TO:
Elemental Science
220 Government Ave., Ste. 7
Niceville, FL 32578
support@elementalscience.com

THE SCIENCE FAIR PROJECT TABLE OF CONTENTS

INTRODUCTION

Introduction: You Can Do This!..7

1. Why you need to do a Science Fair Project.................................9

☞ *What is the scientific method?*   *9*
☞ *What should a science fair project look like?*   *10*
☞ *When should a student do a science fair project?*   *11*

THE STEPS TO COMPLETE A SCIENCE FAIR PROJECT

2. Step 1: Choose a Topic..13

☞ *Decide on an Area of Science*   *13*
☞ *Develop Several Questions About the Area of Science*   *14*
☞ *Choose a Question to be the Topic*   *15*

3. Step 2: Do Some Research..17

☞ *Brainstorm for Research Categories*   *17*
☞ *Research the Categories*   *18*
☞ *Organize the Information*   *20*
☞ *Write a Brief Report*   *20*

4. Step 3: Formulate a Hypothesis...23

☞ *Review the Research*   *23*
☞ *Formulate an Answer*   *24*

5. Step 4: Design an Experiment..25

☞ *Choose a Test*   *26*
☞ *Determine the Variables*   *26*
☞ *Plan the Experiment*   *27*
☞ *Review the Hypothesis*   *28*

6. Step 5: Perform the Experiment...31

☞ *Get Ready for the Experiment*   *31*
☞ *Run the Experiment*   *32*
☞ *Record any Observations and Results*   *32*

7. Step 6: Analyze the Data..35

☞ *Review and Organize the Data*   *35*
☞ *State the Answer*   *36*
☞ *A Quick Word about Theory vs. Fact*   *37*
☞ *Draw Several Conclusions*   *37*

8. Step 7: Create a Board...39

☞ *Plan Out the Board*   *39*
☞ *What kind of board should you use?*   *41*
☞ *Prepare the Information*   *41*
☞ *Put the Board Together*   *43*

9. Step 8: Give a Presentation...45
   ☞ *Prepare the Presentation*   45
   ☞ *Practice the Presentation*   47
   ☞ *Share the Presentation*   47

10. The Science Fair Project for the High School Student...........................49
   ☞ *Increased Independence*   49
   ☞ *In-depth Scientific Research*   50
   ☞ *Increased Complexity of the Experiment Design*   50
   ☞ *What do these changes look like?*   51

APPENDIX

How to Write a Science Fair Project Abstract in Three Easy Steps.......................55
   ☞ *Step 1 - Develop the Words*   55
   ☞ *Step 2 - Write the Draft*   55
   ☞ *Step 3 - Whittle it Down*   56
   ☞ *A Sample Abstract*   56

Sample Science Fair Project Boards...57

STUDENT SHEETS

Step 1: Choose a Topic...61

Step 2: Do Some Research...63

Step 3: Formulate a Hypothesis...69

Step 4: Design an Experiment...71

Step 5: Perform the Experiment...75

Step 6: Analyze the Data...79

Step 7: Create a Board...83

Step 8: Give a Presentation...87

SPECIAL THANKS

We would like to share a special note of thanks to our daughter, Tabitha, who puts up with being the guinea pig for all our projects. We love you sweetheart and are so thankful that we were given the chance to be your parents.

We would also like to extend our gratitude to Audra and Zach, who have graciously allowed us to use the photos of their science fair project boards in this book. You all were the original inspiration for this project and we appreciate you allowing us to help you all these years.

I.
INTRODUCTION: YOU CAN DO THIS!

The science fair project is that dragon in the corner of our basement - back where we keep the science-teaching tools we don't want to use.

We know it's down there. We know we should do something about it. But we really, really don't want to face the idea of having to do a science fair project with our students.

We have no idea where to begin.

And right now, you just want me to tell you that it's okay - you can ignore the dragon and stick to his easier to manage cousin, the hands-on scientific test. Right?

But we are not going to do that. Instead, Brad and I (Paige) going to spend the next ten chapters laying out exactly how to do a science fair project with your students, step by step.

Why are we doing this, you ask?

Because we understand where you are and we both know how critical it is to have someone walk you through the process. My (Paige) first science fair project was a complete disaster. The only direction I got was to come up with a question, design a project to answer it, and then report what I found.

I was confused about how to really go about doing a science fair project and I ended up choosing a terrible topic - Is there a pattern to clouds? In my sixth-grade mind, I was convinced that over a month I would see the same clouds appear again and again in the same repeatable pattern.

Had someone told me to do a bit of research, I would have thrown my question out the window and started over. But, alas, they did not. And I was left with an utter frustration for the science fair project.

So, when it come up the following year, I had a different teacher. Her last name was really hard to pronounce, so we just called her Mrs. I.

Mrs. I walked us through a science fair project step by step. And that year the seed for my passion for science was planted.

When it came time to do a science fair project with our homeschooled students, we developed the following eight steps based on what I remembered from my seventh-grade experience along with Brad's experience in the research lab. And this book is our opportunity to share what we have learned and developed with you.

Take a deep breath.

Head towards the basement.

And let's go down and face that dreaded science fair project dragon together!

1.
WHY YOU NEED TO DO A SCIENCE FAIR PROJECT

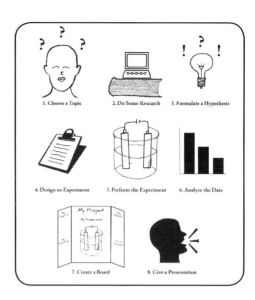

You are at the basement door, but you are not convinced that you should go in. You are not sure that it is really worth the time and effort it takes to do a science fair project.

It's okay. We understand.

Let's chat a bit about what the purpose is behind doing a science fair project. We say that:

> *The purpose of the science fair project is to give the students hands-on experience with the scientific method.*

We know from our research and experience that to truly understand science, one must be familiar with the scientific method. And because of this need, we believe that all students need to have the scientific method demonstrated repeatedly for them. Plus, they need to have used the process over and over again in experiments until it has become a natural habit.

It can take year for the students to fully etch the concept of the scientific method into their mind in such a way that it becomes second nature. The science fair project is an important tool that we, the teacher, can use with our students to increase their understanding and familiarity with the scientific method.

WHAT IS THE SCIENTIFIC METHOD?

If the main purpose of the science fair project is to give our students the opportunity to practice using the scientific method from start to finish, we need to know what the scientific method is in the first place.

Just to make sure we are all on the same page - in a nutshell, the scientific method teaches the brain to logically examine and process all the information it receives.

This method requires that one observes and tests before making a statement of fact. It is the main process that scientists use when asking and answering questions.

The key steps of the scientific method are:

1. Ask a Question
2. Research the Topic
3. Formulate a Hypothesis
4. Test with Experimentation
5. Record and Analyze Observations and Results
6. Draw a Conclusion

When one uses the scientific method, it causes one to look at all the evidence before making a statement of fact.

It can sound like a lofty idea, but in reality, it is an integral part of science education. And if we want our students to be prepared for higher education science, they must be comfortable with this fundamental process.

Are you feeling a bit intimidated?

Please don't!

You are simply teaching your students to take the time to discover the answer to a given problem by using the knowledge they have as well as the things they observe and measure during an experiment.

The scientific method is a simple, yet logical process that follows the same steps every time, and it forms the foundation for the science fair project.

WHAT SHOULD A SCIENCE FAIR PROJECT LOOK LIKE?

In essence the science fair project is an in-depth experiment which will take several weeks to complete. It follows the steps of the scientific method from start to finish, but adds to more steps to help the students share what they have learned.

Our eight steps to complete the science fair project are as follows:

- **Step 1** - Choose a Topic
- **Step 2** - Do Some Research
- **Step 3** - Formulate a Hypothesis
- **Step 4** - Design an Experiment
- **Step 5** - Perform Experiment
- **Step 6** - Analyze Data
- **Step 7** - Create a Board
- **Step 8** - Give Presentation

We'll break each of these steps into manageable chunks in the coming chapters. But, basically, once a school year, your older students should follow these steps to complete a science fair project.

Their projects should work through the scientific method from beginning to end. The first time the students do this, you will need to be certain to thoroughly explain each step and coach them through the entire process. They will need you to work alongside of them as an advisor from the time they formulate their question until they polish up their presentation. This is so that they learn the process correctly from the beginning. But, as the students become more familiar with the process, they will be able to do more of the work on their own.

It is also important to have the students present their project to a group and answer related questions from them. This will serve to reinforce what they have learned as well as help them to discern how to communicate what they know.

The best way to achieve this is to have the students participate in a Science Fair where their project will be judged, but if that's not possible for your student, don't skip this component. The students can still present his project to his family or a group of his peers.

WHEN SHOULD A STUDENT DO A SCIENCE FAIR PROJECT?

The students doing a science fair project should be able to read fairly well on their own. They should also be able to summarize what they have learned from reading several paragraphs of non-fiction material. And, they should be starting to learn how to apply what they have learned to a new situation that is before them.

For these reasons, we recommend beginning to do a science fair project with your students once they are in fifth grade and continuing to do so through middle school. Your goal is to do at least three science fair projects with your students.

As the students progress into high school, the science fair project is still a beneficial tool, especially for the student who wants to continue on in the sciences. However, it is not as critical to do a science fair project with your students past the middle school years. (*Please see chapter 10 for a more thorough explanation of how to use the science fair project with the high school student.*)

CONCLUSION

The science fair project is a key tool in our science-teaching kit.

It is an essential component of an excellent science education for middle school students. These students need to experience the scientific method from start to finish in a real and practical way.

In the next eight chapters, we will explain each step in detail so that you will be prepared to guide your students through this much maligned and often misunderstood process.

2.
STEP 1: CHOOSE A TOPIC

The first step of the science fair project is to choose a topic for the project. What you will do in this step is patterned after the first step of the scientific method, which is "Ask a Question".

The first step of the scientific method begins when the scientist observes an occurrence that makes him wonder what is happening. Then, he creates a question which relates to what originally peaked his interest. When crafting this inquiry, the scientist will make sure that the question is worded in such a way that he will be able to measure whether or not he has obtained the answer.

For this step, your students should:

- Begin with deciding on an area of science that interests them.
- Develop several questions about this area of science which they want to answer.
- And, finally, choose one of those questions to be the topic for their project.

Let's take a closer look at how this process works!

DECIDE ON AN AREA OF SCIENCE

The first part of completing step one of the science fair project is to decide on an area of science that interests the students.

The students should choose an area that fascinates them, something in science that they want to know more about. Because if they are interested in the area, it will be much easier for them to complete the project and they will be more likely to engage with the material.

Here is what you need to do:

✓ Begin by leading the students to brainstorm about things in science that interest them.

13

✓ Next, have them rank these areas by degree of interest.

✓ Then, have them choose one area on which to focus.

If their area is too broad, you will want them to narrow their area down a bit. You can do this by asking them what they find interesting about the particular field.

For example, let's say a student has written the following for his brainstorm list:

> plants

> animals

> light bulbs

> magnets

He decides that he is most fascinated with plants. Plants are quite a broad topic, so to narrow it down a bit you ask him:

What is it about plants that you find interesting?

He says that he is most interested in the way that plants grow. So, he writes down the following for the area of science he would like to explore with his science fair project:

> the growth of plants

And you are ready to move onto the next part of this step.

DEVELOP SEVERAL QUESTIONS ABOUT THE AREA OF SCIENCE

Once the students have determined their area of science, they need to develop several questions about the subject that they can answer with their project.

Remember that good questions begin with how, what, when, who, which, why or where.

Here is what you need to do:

✓ Say to the students, "Now that we have determined the area of science we want to learn about, let's think of some question that we want to answer about the subject."

At this point, you are getting them to think of possible questions they could answer, you will narrow down these questions in the next section.

So, let's rejoin our sample student who chose the growth of the plants as his area of science. For this section, he could come up with questions like:

> Why do plants grow?

> How fast do plants grow?

> When do plants grow?

> Which plants grow faster?

Once, the students have several options for questions, you are ready to move onto the final section of this step.

CHOOSE A QUESTION TO BE THE TOPIC

Now that the students have several options of questions they can answer with their science fair project, you will need to have them choose one of those questions for their project.

Some of their questions will be easy to develop an experiment for their science fair project that will determine the answer; some will not. If their question is too broad, you will need to help them narrow it down to something more specific.

Let's analyze one of the questions our sample student came up with:

> Why do plants grow?

This question is too broad because sunlight, water and nutrients all affect plant growth, not to mention the weather and a whole host of other factors. It will be far too time-consuming to do an experiment that will measure the answer to this question.

So, you will want to help the student narrow down the question. Some options would be:

- How does the lack of sunlight affect the growth of house plants?
- Which soil is best for house plants to be grown in?

Each of these questions is more specific, making them far easier for the student to measure.

It is important to note that the student may need to tweak and adjust their topical question as they proceed through the next several steps.

They may find through their research that they need to be more specific. Or, they may discover as they design their experiment that their question needs to be a little less specific. Their topic remains a fluid question until they begin their experiment.

CONCLUSION

The keys for choosing a topic are to start with deciding on an area of science, then to develop several questions about that area, and finally to choose a question to be the topic of the project.

Once the students have their topic chosen, they will move onto Step 2: Do Some Research.

But before we move on, we wanted to mention to you that we have developed worksheets you can use with your students as you complete each step.

3.
STEP 2: DO SOME RESEARCH

Remember that fruitless cloud science fair project from the introduction? All that hassle could have been avoided if Paige would have just done this step before beginning her project.

The second step of the science fair project is to do some research. This process is based on the second step of the scientific method.

In this step of the method, the scientist researches about the topic from the question so that he will have some background knowledge about the subject, which will give him a basis for formulating his hypothesis. You see, it is very hard for someone to predict what is going to happen in an experiment without knowing something about the principles at work. The scientist also does research to prevent him from repeating mistakes that have been made in the past.

For the science fair project, the students also need to do some research so that they can make an educated guess on the answer to their question. This research will also be useful to them when they design their experiment.

For this step, your students should:

- Begin by brainstorming for categories that are relevant to their topical question.
- Research these categories at home through their personal library, through the Internet and their local library.
- And, finally, organize the information into a brief report.

Let's take a closer look at how this process works!

BRAINSTORM FOR RESEARCH CATEGORIES

The first part of this step of the science fair project begins with the student brainstorming for categories to research. They need to develop relevant research categories before they begin to search for information as this will help the student to maintain a more focused approach to their research.

This key will help the student to know where to begin their research and to know what information is important to their project and what is not. It's an important organizational tool that you should not skip.

You will need to guide your student through the brainstorming process, just like you did in step 1. However, if your student is younger, you may need to hold his hand through this process even more, since the younger student may have a harder time coming up with categories that relate to their topic.

The students should have at least three categories and no more than five. This will help them obtain relevant information as well as make it easier for them to write their report.

Once the students have chosen their research categories, have them assign each category a number.

Let go back to our sample student, who chose the topical question, "Which soil is best for house plants to be grown in?" He could then come up with the follow topics to research:

> What is found in soil
> Plant growth
> General information about plant structure
> Types of soil

Once the students have their research categories, they are ready to move onto the next part of this step.

RESEARCH THE CATEGORIES

Now, the students are ready to begin their research!

Have the students begin by looking at reference material that they have close at hand, such as encyclopedias that they own or that are in the classroom. Then, they can look to their local library or the Internet for additional information. Depending upon their experience with research, you may or may not have to walk them through this entire process.

We recommend that the students use a pack of index cards on which to write their information.

As they uncover bit of relevant data, have them write each fact in their own words on a separate index card. Have them number each card at the top left with the category in which it fits, which will make them easier to organize.

We also recommend that they assign a letter for each reference they use, which they can write in the right-hand top corner of each card. This way, after they organize and sort their cards, they will know which reference they need to include in their bibliography!

So, their index cards would look like the one below:

Category Number	Reference Letter
One piece of Information	

The students will gather a lot of information from their research and it may seem like a waste of index cards, but it is important that they follow this procedure as it will help them organize their research. In the next key, you are going to help them to sort through what they have found and to determine what is relevant for their project and what is not.

Back to our sample student who is interested in how plants grow. He is researching four different categories and has found a book all about soil, which he labels as reference B.

He finds out that there are several different types of soil, such as sand, silt, clay, loam, peat and chalk.

From another reference, which he labeled reference G, he discovered that a good portion of the world's sandy soil is found in the Great Sahara Desert.

So, he would add two cards to his stack that would look like the following cards:

4	B
There are several different types of soil, such as sand, silt, clay, loam, peat and chalk.	

4	G
A good portion of the world's sandy soil is found in the Great Sahara Desert.	

And once he has a stack of index cards, you are ready to move onto the next part of the second step of the science fair project.

ORGANIZE THE INFORMATION

Once the students have finished their research, you need to have them organize and sort through the information that they have found.

Here is what you need to do:

✓ Begin by having the students sort their cards into piles using their research categories, which are in the top left hand of their index card.

✓ Then, have the student read through each fact and determine five to seven of the most relevant facts from each pile. You may need to help them determine which facts are relevant to their project (i.e. useful for answering their topical question) and which ones are not. These facts will form the basis of their report for the next key.

So, our example student has sorted his cards into four piles according to his research categories. He has chosen six relevant facts from each pile except the fourth one.

He has been able to choose six facts for his fourth category so far, but he can't decide which of the facts we shared above about soil that he should include. Remember that his topical question was: Which soil is best for house plants to be grown in?

In this case, he should discard the fact about sand and the Great Sahara Desert because the information about the different types of soil is far more relevant to his particular question.

Now that the students are organized, you are ready to move onto the final part of this step.

WRITE A BRIEF REPORT

The final key to the second step of the science fair project is to have the students write a brief report sharing what they have learned.

This report should be one to two pages in length and should contain three to five paragraphs. This will be an easy task for the students because the previous sections have prepared them for this task.

Here is what you need to do:

✓ Begin by having the students determine the order they want to share their research categories. Normally they would go from broad information about their subject to more specific information for their project.

✓ After they do this they need to take the five to seven facts from the first category and write a three to four sentence paragraph by combing the facts into a coherent passage.

✓ Have the students repeat this process until they have a three to five paragraph paper.

✓ Then, the students will need to edit and revise their paper so that it because a cohesive report.

✓ Finally, they will need to add in a bibliography with their sources after their report.

Our sample student chose to organize his research categories like this:

> General information about plant structure (#3)
> Plant growth (#2)

> What is found in soil (#1)

> Types of soil (#4)

Then he writes his first paragraph from his stack of cards, which looks like this:

> The group of plants that I am looking at in my project is called vascular plants. This means that they use a system of tubes to transport nutrients and water throughout the plant. Vascular plants all conduct photosynthesis, which happens at the cellular level. These plants also all have roots for drawing up water and nutrients, stems for transporting those nutrients, leaves for photosynthesis and flowers for reproduction.

His final report could look something like this:

> The type of plant that I am looking at in my project is called a vascular plant. This means that they use a system of tubes to transport nutrients and water throughout the plant. Vascular plants all conduct photosynthesis, which happens at the cellular level. These plants also all have roots, stems, leaves and flowers.
>
> Vascular plants grow by drawing up nutrients from the soil and using them to make energy from the sun. The roots of a vascular plant draw water and nutrients from the surrounding soil. The stem of the vascular plant takes the food up to the leaves. In the leaves, a process, called photosynthesis, uses sunlight to turn the food into energy. The plant uses this energy to grow.
>
> Since vascular plants get their food from the soil, they need it to grow. They also need soil because it gives them a place to anchor themselves. Soil traps the water and air that plants need for growth. Finally, soil gives a place for nutrients and minerals to attach to and the roots of the plant can extract this food.
>
> Soil is made up of rocks, minerals and decaying plants or animals. Most types of soil are a combination of these materials, which allows for variety in how the soils hold water and nutrients. There are several types of soil, such as sand, silt, clay, loam, peat and chalk. Generally, sand is very porous, with lots of space for water and nutrients, while clay is very dense. In my experiment, I am going to see what type of soil is best for growing grass.

CONCLUSION

The keys for researching the science fair project are to brainstorm for research categories, to research the categories, to organize the information and to write a brief report.

Once the students have finished their report, they are ready to move onto Step 3: Formulating a Hypothesis.

4.
STEP 3: FORMULATE A HYPOTHESIS

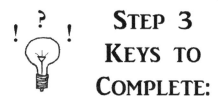

STEP 3 KEYS TO COMPLETE:

1. Review the research.

2. Formulate the answer.

At this point our students are excited about the topic for their project and they have done a bit of research to gain an idea of what the answer to their question could be.

The third step of the science fair project is to formulate a hypothesis. This process is patterned after step three of the scientific method, in which the scientist formulates his hypothesis.

A hypothesis is an educated guess about the answer to a question. The scientist will formulate their educated guess in such a way that he will able to test the validity of his statement. He will do this so that he can measure whether or not he has obtained the answer to his original question. Because of this, hypotheses are typically simple "if-then" statements that are not more than one sentence long.

At this point in the science fair project process, your students are ready to make their educated guesses about the answer to their questions. So, this step will be relatively easy because the students have been well-prepared.

For this step, your students should:

- Begin by reviewing all of their research and their question.
- Then, formulate an answer to their project's question.

Let's take a closer look at how this process works!

REVIEW THE RESEARCH

The first part of step three of the science fair project begins with the students reviewing their research. The idea is to have the information that they have learned to be fresh in their minds.

Here is what you need to do:

✓ Have the students read over their report or have them read over each of the index cards they made.

The level of involvement for this key will depend on how much time goes by between step two and step three of the science fair project.

FORMULATE AN ANSWER

After the students have reviewed their research, they should also read over their question one more time. Once all the information is fresh in their minds, they are ready to make an educated guess at the answer to their question.

Here is what you need to do:

✓ Guide them to craft a response in the form of an "if-then" statement that they will be able to design an experiment to test.

However, keep in mind that not all questions can be answered easily with if-then statements. As they design their experiment in the next step, you can still have them make a few adjustments to their hypothesis, if necessary.

So, let's go back to sample student who chose the question, "Which soil is best for house plants to be grown in?" He has done his research and found out that plants depend upon soil for water and nutrients. He believes that the more loam the soil has in it, the more nutrients it will hold. Therefore, the better the plant will grow.

So, his hypothesis might look like one of the following options:

> If a plant is grown in a potting soil, then it will grow much faster.
> I believe that plants grown in potting soil will grow better than plants grown in other types of soil.

CONCLUSION

The keys to completing the hypothesis step of the science fair project are to review the research and to formulate an answer.

Once the students have formulated a hypothesis that answers their topical question, they are ready to move onto Step 4: Design an Experiment.

5.
STEP 4: DESIGN AN EXPERIMENT

STEP 4 KEYS TO COMPLETE:

1. Choose a Test.

2. Determine the Variables.

3. Plan the Experiment.

4. Review the Hypothesis.

Roll up your sleeves - it is time for the nitty gritty fun to begin!

The fourth step of the science fair project is to design an experiment. This process is patterned after step four of the scientific method, in which the scientist develops and performs an experiment that will test whether his hypothesis is true or false.

It is important for the test to be fair, so the scientist will only change one variable at a time and he will always have a control group. Generally, he will have more than one sample in each group which makes his findings much more reliable. The scientist may also find that several experiments are necessary to thoroughly prove whether or not his hypothesis is correct, but don't worry, we won't be that detailed with our science fair experiments!

At this point in the process, our students have a chosen a topic, done some research and formulated their hypotheses. Now, they are ready to design their experiment!

The students may find this step to be a bit challenging, but a well-planned experiment design will yield reliable results. So, it is important that you take the time to walk the students through this process.

For this step, your students should:

- Begin by brainstorming for possible ways to test their hypotheses and choosing one of those methods for their experiment.
- Determine their variables.
- Plan their experiment around one of the methods of testing.
- And then, review their hypotheses to make sure that their experiment design will prove their statement true or false.

Let's take a closer look at how this process works!

CHOOSE A TEST

Step four of the science fair project begins with the students brainstorming for possible ways to test their hypotheses statements.

Here is what you need to do:

✓ Ask the students, "What kind of a test could you use that would answer your question and prove your hypothesis either true or false?"

✓ Have the students write down each idea they have, but keep in mind that they may need a fair amount of help with this process.

If the students find that they cannot come up with any options for testing their hypotheses, they may need to tweak their statements a bit. If they decide to do this, make sure they verify that the new versions still answer their original topical questions.

Once the students have written down several ideas, have them review the options and choose one of the ideas for their projects.

Let's go back to our sample student. He could come up with the following ideas for his experiment:

> I could grow a whole bunch of different kinds of plants in sand to see which one would grow the best.

> I could grow one type of plant in several types of soil to see which one would grow the best.

> I could grow several different kinds of plants in several different kinds of soil to see which one would grow the best.

The first option does not really test to see if his hypothesis is true, since it tests the growth of different types of plants in the same soil rather than how the types of soil would affect the growth of those plants.

His third option takes care of the problems in the first, but this experiment would be very involved and would probably take more time than the middle school student has. This option could work for a high school student that has planned to devote several months to his project.

For our purposes, the most logical choice is the second option as it will verify the accuracy of the his hypothesis. Plus, it will also be the easiest experiment test to set-up and perform.

DETERMINE THE VARIABLES

Now that your students have chosen a method to test their hypotheses, they need to determine the variables that will exist in their test.

There are two main types of variables at play in any experiment - independent variables and dependent variables. Let's take a closer look at each.

The independent variable is the factor that is controlled or changed by the scientist performing the experiment. The dependent variable is the factor being tested in the experiment. The dependent variable is what the scientist uses to measure the effect of the changes to the independent variable. In other words, the dependent variable depends upon the independent variable.

It is also important to us to mention controlled variables, which are factors that are not being examined in the experiment. A scientist will keep the controlled variables constant so that their effect on the test will be minimized.

Once the students understand the different types of variables, they will need to determine the factors that are at play in their experiment. You can have them answer the following questions to help them see what their variables are:

- What factor am I trying to test? (Independent variable)
- What factor will I use to measure the progress of the test? (Dependent variable)
- What factors do I need to keep constant so that they will not affect my results? (Controlled variables)

After the students have answered these questions, have them write down their independent, dependent and controlled variables. Middle school students should have only one independent variable and one dependent variable in their science fair project experiments.

For example, our sample student has chosen to test his hypothesis by growing grass in several different types of soil. Here is what he would write down for the variables in his experiment:

> Independent Variable - The type of soil
> Dependent Variable - The growth of the plant
> Controlled Variables - The amount of sunlight, the amount of water, the size of the pot, the type of grass, and the nutrients in the soil.

Once your students have determined the variables for their experiment, you are ready to move onto the next part of this step.

PLAN THE EXPERIMENT

Now that the students understand the variables that are at work, they are ready to use this information along with their testing idea to create an experiment design.

Here is what you need to do:

✓ Explain to the students the parameters of their experiments. (i.e., they must have a control group as well as several test groups, the control group will have nothing changed, while each of the test groups will have only one change to the independent variable, and the students should also plan on having several samples in each of their test groups.)

✓ Have the students formulate a plan by determining what their test groups will be and deciding how long they have to run their test.

✓ Once they have this information, have the students write out their experiment design.

Here is what our sample student's test groups could look like:

> Control Group - a six inch pot with soil from my backyard

> Test Group #1 - a six inch pot with potting soil

> Test Group #2 - a six inch pot with sand

Next, he chooses to use a grass seed blend from the local hardware store as his plant in the experiment, which he notes will take up to two weeks to germinate. He decides that he wants to measure at least two weeks of growth, so he will need four weeks for his experiment.

Now, he sits down and comes up with this plan:

I will begin by filling three pots with soil from my backyard, which I will call my control group. Then, I will fill three more pots with potting soil from the store, which I will call test group #1. Finally, I will fill three more pots with sand from the sand box, which I will call test group #2.

Next, I will plant one tablespoon of grass seed in each pot. I will water each of the pots with a nutrient rich solution made from fertilizer and water on the first day. After that, I will set each of the pots on a window sill in full sunlight. I will check the pots every day for four weeks and water them with the nutrient rich solution when the soil appears dry. Once I notice that the plants have sprouted, I will record how much they grow each day until the end.

Once your students have a plan for their experiment, there is just one more thing to do for this step.

REVIEW THE HYPOTHESIS

Now that the students have designed their experiment, they need go back and make sure that their test will prove their hypotheses true or false.

Here is what you need to do:

✓ Have the students to read over their hypotheses and their experiment design.

✓ Ask them, if you got this result from your experiment, would that prove your hypothesis true or false? You may have to ask this type of question several times to verify that their experiment design is sound.

So, for our sample student's science fair project, he would read over his hypothesis and his experiment design. Then, you could ask the following question:

If you find that the plants in the potting soil grow five inches taller than the control group, would it prove your hypothesis true or false?

Your student should say yes, which means that they now have a possible valid experiment design.

CONCLUSION

The keys to designing the experiment for the science fair project are to choose a test, determine the variables, plan the experiment and review the hypothesis.

Once the students have a verified experiment design on paper, they are ready to move onto Step 5: Perform the Experiment.

6.
STEP 5: PERFORM THE EXPERIMENT

STEP 5 KEYS TO COMPLETE:

1. Get ready for the experiment.

2. Run the experiment.

3. Record any observations and results.

Pull out your lab coat and goggles - if you have them - it's time to get dirty!

The fifth step of the science fair project is to perform the experiment. This process is patterned after step four and five of the scientific method, in which the scientist develops and performs an experiment and records the results from that experiment.

This step may take the scientist several weeks or several years, depending upon how involved his experiment is and how many trials he may need to run. But during the entire experiment, he will record all his observations and measure his results. The scientist will wait until the experiment has come to a close before he analyzes the data that he collects.

At this point in the science fair project process, the students have completed their design and are now ready to perform their experiment. This step may take several weeks depending on how long they have designed their trial.

For this step, your students should:

- Get ready for their experiment by gathering and preparing their supplies.
- Run their experiment from start to finish using the plan they developed in the last step.
- Record their observations and results as the test progresses.

Let's take a closer look at how this process works!

GET READY FOR THE EXPERIMENT

The fifth step of the science fair project begins with a bit of preparation. The students already have a plan in place, but there are still a few things they need to do before beginning their experiment.

Here is what you need to have the students do:

✓ Look at a calendar and make sure that they will be home for the duration of the trial because they will need to be there to make observations and record results on each day of testing.

✓ Gather and prep any materials that they will be using during their experiment.

So back to our sample student - he will need to block out four weeks where he will be able to check the project daily. He will also need to gather potting soil, sand, soil from his yard, nine pots, fertilizer, and grass seed. Finally, he will need to mix up his nutrient rich solution using the directions on the back of the fertilizer he purchased.

RUN THE EXPERIMENT

This is where the fun of the science fair project really begins!

The students have done a lot of work to reach this point, but that preparation has paved a smooth road for their experiment. At this point they are familiar with their research and their design, so they should be able to carry out their testing with little to no help.

Here is what you need to do:

✓ Have the students write down a list of things they need to check each day during the experiment.

Be sure that they include taking pictures of what they see during their experiment on their list as they will need these images for their project board.

For example, our sample student's list could include the following:

> Take pictures of the plants every day
> Make daily observations about each of the groups of pots in the experiment
> Once the grass begins to grow, measure and record how much it has grown
> Check the soil daily for moisture, add water if needed
> Rotate the pots every week so that both sides receive equal exposure to the sun

RECORD ANY OBSERVATIONS AND RESULTS

As the students run their experiment, they need to compile their observations and results.

Observations are the record of the things the scientist sees happening in an experiment, while results are specific and measurable. Observations are generally recorded in journal form, while results can be compiled into tables, charts or graphs.

Here is what you need to do:

✓ Help the students create a table to record their results.

✓ Provide them with a journal for their observations.

✓ Once they finish their experiment, assist them in creating a chart or graph with their data.

It is important to note that at this point the students are not interpreting the results of their experiment. The analysis and interpretation of the data will be done in the next step. For now, they are simply relaying and recording information on what has happened during their experiment.

Let's go back to the student we have been discussing. He has kept a journal of his observations during the experiment. His journal contained entries like the two examples below:

Day 8 – The grass in the pots from test group #1 and the control group has finally sprouted. The pots of test group #2 look like they might sprout tomorrow. I had to water the pots in test group 1 today.

Day 17 – The grass in the test group #1 pots has grown the tallest so far, this is followed by test group #2 and then the control group. All of the pots have grass that is looking green and healthy. I had to water the pots in test group #1 and #2 today.

He also measured how much the plants had grown each day and then plotted each of his measurements on a graph that looks like this:

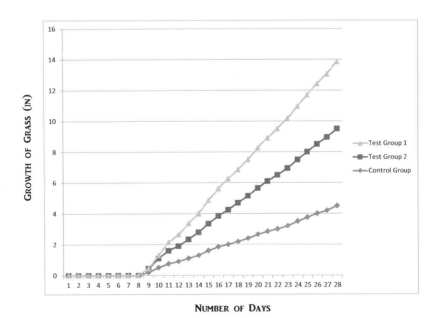

NUMBER OF DAYS

Once your students have finished their experiment and have collected their data, you are ready to move onto the next step.

CONCLUSION

The keys to performing the experiment for the science fair project are to get ready for the experiment, to run the experiment and to record any observations and results made during the experiment.

Once the students have finished their experiment, they are ready to move onto Step 6: Analyze the Data.

7.
STEP 6:
ANALYZE THE DATA

STEP 6 KEYS TO COMPLETE:

1. Review and organize the data.

2. State the answer.

3. Draw several conclusions.

Now, we get to figure out what is what!

The sixth step of the science fair project is to analyze the data. This process is patterned after step five and six of the scientific method, in which the scientist analyzes what he has observed and recorded so that he can make a statement about whether or not his hypothesis was true.

The scientist's statement will communicate his results to other scientists and hopefully answer his original question. The scientist may find that his hypothesis was false or that his experiment design did not really answer his question. If this is the case, he will formulate a new hypothesis and begin the process again until he is able to answer his question.

Our students have finished their experiments and are ready to analyze the data they have collected.

For this step, your students should:

- Begin this process by reviewing and organizing the information they have collected.
- State the answer to their original question which they discovered through their testing.
- And, finally, draw several conclusions detailing what they have learned through their experiment.

Let's take a closer look at how this process works!

REVIEW AND ORGANIZE THE DATA

During their experiment, the students recorded observations and measured results. Remember that observations are a record of the things seen during the trial, while the results are the specific and measurable data collected during the testing. Now, in this step the students need to analyze this information to determine if their hypotheses are true or false.

Here is what you need to have them do:

✓ Read over each of their journal entries and note any trends in their observations.

✓ Interpret the charts or graphs they created in the last step and write down the information that they can glean from them.

For the sample project we have been discussing, the student notes the following trends from his observation journal:

> All of the plants were healthy throughout the test.

> The grass in test group #1 appeared to grow quicker than test group #2 and the control group.

> The pots in test group #2 were water the most frequently.

He also recognizes the following information from his results:

> The grass in test group #1 grew the best.

> The grass is test group #2 grew better than the grass in the control group.

STATE THE ANSWER

Now that the students have noted trends from their observations and interpreted information from their results, they can use this data to answer their question.

Here is what you need to have them do:

✓ Determine if they have proved their hypotheses true or false. If the students are unable to determine the validity of their statements, they will need to go back and do some additional testing. Generally, if a scientist finds that his hypothesis was proven false, he will go back and perform more tests before stating the answer to his original question. However, the middle school student undertaking the science fair project does not need to do this. If your students find that their hypotheses have been proven false, simply have them note this in their conclusion.

✓ Craft a one sentence answer to their original topical questions from step one. Their statements should begin with, "I found that ___" or "I discovered that ___." In the rare case that the students are unable to state an answer to their question, they need to take what they have learned, go back to the drawing table and redesign their experiment.

Our sample student is able to see from his journal entries and from the graph he created that his hypothesis was proven true. Remember that his original question was, "Which soil is best for house plants to be grown in?"

In this part of the process, he states the following as an answer to his question:

I discovered that the house plants in my experiment grew best in potting soil.

It is important to note that the student is theorizing that potting soil is the best medium for growing house plants. This is why he needs to begin his statement with, "I discovered" and use the phrase "in my experiment."

If he wanted to make a statement of fact, such as, "House plants grow best in potting soil", he would need to run quite a few more trials. There are additional types of soil that he did not test and other factors involved in a house plant's growth that he did not consider. So, additional experiments need to be done before the student can make a statement of fact about the answer to his question.

The high school student interested in the sciences should set aside the time to do this kind of testing, but the middle school student completing a science fair project does not need to go any further.

A QUICK WORD ABOUT THEORY VS. FACT

What is the difference between a theory and a fact?

To answer this question, we must examine the origins of the words themselves.

The word theory comes from the ancient Greek word *theoria*, which means "a looking at, viewing or beholding." In science, a theory is an analytical tool used for understanding, explaining or predicting cause for a certain subject matter.

The word "fact" comes from the Latin word *factum*, which means "a thing done or performed." In science, a fact is an objective truth that can be seen in nature or confirmed through repeated experiments.

So, we can say that theories are meant to be tested by experimentation and observation to determine if they are facts, while facts are truths that can be verified through repeatable experimentation or by real-time observations.

And with that out of the way, let's chat about the last part of this step.

DRAW SEVERAL CONCLUSIONS

When the students draw conclusions, they are putting into words what they have learned from their project.

Here is what you need to make sure that they include in their conclusion:

✓ The answer to their question
✓ Whether or not their hypotheses were proven true (*If their hypotheses were proven false, they should state why.*)
✓ Any problems or difficulties they ran into while performing their experiment
✓ Anything interesting they discovered that they would like to share
✓ Ways that they would like to expand their experiment in the future

This conclusion should be one paragraph, or about four to six sentences, in length. Have the students begin their concluding paragraph with the statement they wrote for the previous key.

Our sample student could have written the following conclusion:

I discovered that the house plants in my experiment grew best in potting soil. This finding proved my hypothesis to be true. I also found it interesting that the plants in test group #2 had to be watered more than the other pots. In the future, I would like to test how water affects plant growth or how much moisture different types of soil can hold.

CONCLUSION

The keys to analyzing the data for the science fair project are to review and organize the data, to state the answer and to draw several conclusions.

Once the students have detailed what they have learned from their experiment, they are ready to move onto Step 7: Create a Board.

8.
STEP 7:
CREATE
A BOARD

STEP 7 KEYS TO COMPLETE:

1. Plan out the board.

2. Prepare the information.

3. Put the board together.

It's time for your students to get ready to show off what they have discovered!

The seventh step of the science fair project is to create a board. This process is not patterned after any step of the scientific method, but rather it gives the students a chance to graphically communicate what they have learned from their project.

The board created in this step will serve as the visual aid for their science fair presentation, so it's important that it be eye-catching and attractive.

For this step, the students should:

- Plan out and prepare the information for their board in this step.
- Pull all of the information and design elements together and put them onto each panel in preparation for presenting their project.

Let's take a closer look at how this process works!

PLAN OUT THE BOARD

The science fair project board is the visual representation of the students' hard work, so you definitely want them to put as much effort into this step as they have into the others. The board will have specific sections that are set, but the students should feel free to personalize the look of their project boards with color and graphics that suit their tastes.

These boards should have a large center section with two smaller flaps on either side and be able to stand on a table so that they can display their board as they give their presentation.

Here is what you need to have them do:

- ✓ Plan where they are going to put their information.
- ✓ Decide on what color scheme they are going to use.
- ✓ Choose what graphics they will use to highlight their project.

The students will prepare and revise their information for their project boards in the next section. But before we get to that, we wanted to share with you a list of what information needs to be included along with where it is typically found on the project board. The students can certainly mix things up a bit, but be sure to remind them that their information needs to be placed in such a way that it is easy for someone else to follow the progression.

THE LEFT SECTION OF THE BOARD TYPICALLY HAS:

- **Introduction** – This includes their question and a brief explanation of why they chose that topic.
- **Hypothesis** – This is their educated guess from step three.
- **Research** – This is the report that the students wrote in step two.

THE CENTER SECTION OF THE BOARD TYPICALLY HAS:

- **Materials** – This is a list of the supplies used in the project.
- **Procedure** – This is a brief explanation of what was done for the experiment.
- **Pictures, Graphs, and Charts from the Experiment** –These are visual representations of the project.

  Note—If you have a highly visual project, you could place the materials and procedure sections on the right flap instead.

THE RIGHT SECTION OF THE BOARD TYPICALLY HAS:

- **Results** – This includes the trends from the observations and the interpretation of the results.
- **Conclusions** – This is the concluding paragraph from the previous step.

The students can also display a portion of their project or a photo album with pictures from their experiment on the table in front of their board.

For the science fair project we have been discussing, our sample student could also plan to display one pot from each of his test groups in front of his board.

The student could come up with the following plan for his project board:

WHAT KIND OF BOARD SHOULD YOU USE?

Before we move onto the nitty gritty job of preparing the information for the board, let us chat about the kind of board you will need. You are looking for the following:

✓ A tri-fold board that is at least 36" high and 48" wide,

✓ A board with the two side sections that fold into the center section.

If you search the internet for science fair project boards, you will find plenty of options, some with header boards, some not. You can usually purchase a project board at most local Walmart, Target, or Michael's.

PREPARE THE INFORMATION

The students have put in a lot of effort until this point, but the work they have done in the previous steps will make it easier for them to prepare the information for their board. The students need to type the information up and choose a font and font size for their board.

Here is a list of what you need to have the students prepare:

✓ **The Introduction** – Have the students turning their question from step one into a statement. Then, they should write two to three more sentences explaining why they chose their specific topic. The students should end their introductory paragraph by sharing the question that they were trying to answer with their project.

41

✓ **The Hypothesis** – Have the students type up and prepare their hypotheses from step three for the project board.

✓ **The Research** – Have the students type up and prepare their research report from step two for the project board.

✓ **The Materials** – Have the students type up a list of the materials they used for their project.

✓ **The Procedure** – Have the students revise the experiment design they wrote in step four so that it is written in the past tense.

✓ **The Results** – Have the student turn the trends in the observations they noted and the results they interpreted in step six into a paragraph.

✓ **The Conclusion** – Have the students type up and prepare their concluding paragraph from step six for the project board.

Our sample student could have written the following for his project:

- **The Introduction**

    I wanted to know what kind of soil is best for house plants to grow in. I enjoy having plants on my window sill, but they do not always grow a lot. So, I wanted to know if the type of soil that they are planted in makes a difference in how much they grow. For this reason, I choose to answer the question: Which soil is best for house plants to be grown in?

- **The Hypothesis**

    My hypothesis was, if a plant is grown in a potting soil, then it will grow much faster.

- **The Research**

    House plants are vascular plants. They grow by drawing up nutrients from the soil and using them to make energy from the sun. The roots of a vascular plant draw water and nutrients from the surrounding soil. The stem of the vascular plant takes the food up to the leaves. In the leaves, a process called photosynthesis uses sunlight to turn the food into energy. The plant uses this energy to grow.

    Since vascular plants get their food from the soil, they need it to grow. They also need soil because it gives them a place to anchor themselves. Soil traps the water and air that plants need for growth. Finally, soil gives a place for nutrients and minerals to attach to and the roots of the plant can extract this food.

    Soil is made up of rocks, minerals and decaying plants or animals. Most types of soil are a combination of these materials, which allows for variety in how the soils hold water and nutrients. There are several types of soil, such as sand, silt, clay, loam, peat and chalk. Generally, sand is very porous, with lots of space for water and nutrients, while clay is very dense.

- **The Materials**
    > Nine pots
    > Grass seed

> Potting soil

> Sand

> Dirt from outdoors

> Miracle Grow

> Water

- **The Procedure**

    I began by filling three pots with soil from my backyard, which I called my control group. Then, I filled three more pots with potting soil from the store, which I called test group #1. Finally, I filled three more pots with sand from the sand box, which I called test group #2.

    After that I planted one tablespoon of grass seed in each pot. On the first day, I watered each of the pots with a nutrient rich solution made from Miracle Grow fertilizer and water. After that, I set all of the pots on a window sill in full sunlight. I checked the pots every day over four weeks and watered them with the nutrient rich solution when the soil appeared to be dry. Once I noticed that the plants had sprouted, I started to record how much they had grown each day until the end of my experiment.

- **The Results**

    During my experiment, I observed that all of the plants were healthy throughout the test. I noticed that the grass in test group #1 grew the best and that the grass is test group #2 grew better than the grass in the control group. This was confirmed when my results showed that the pots in test group #1 grew four and a half inches taller than the grass in test group #2 and that the pots in test group #2 grew five inches taller than the grass in the control group.

- **The Conclusion**

    I discovered that the house plants in my experiment grew best in potting soil. This finding proved my hypothesis to be true. I also found it interesting that the plants in test group #2 had to be watered more than the other pots. In the future, I would like to test how water affects plant growth or how much moisture different types of soil can hold.

PUT THE BOARD TOGETHER

At this point, the students have planned out their project board and prepared the information they need for their boards. The final step to create their boards is to pull it all together!

Here is what you need to have them do:

- ✓ Cut out the decorative elements and glue them to the backboard.
- ✓ Print and cut out their informational paragraphs. (*For added depth, they can glue their paragraphs onto foam board before adding the information to their project board.*)

✓ Add their title and the finishing touches to their board. (*This title can be the student's question or they can make up a new title that reflects the purpose of their experiment.*)

Please see Appendix page 57 for a couple of pictures of actual project boards to help you understand what the finished product can look like.

CONCLUSION

The keys to creating a board for the science fair project are to plan out the board, to prepare the information for the board and to put the board together.

Once the students have finished their project board, they are ready to move onto Step 8: Give a Presentation.

9.
STEP 8: GIVE A PRESENTATION

STEP 8 KEYS TO COMPLETE:

1. Prepare the presentation.

2. Practice the presentation.

3. Share the presentation.

Now your students have the honor of sharing all their hard work with a group of people! They have done a lot of work up until this point, so they should be very familiar with their projects, which will make this step so much easier.

The eighth step of the science fair project is to give a presentation. This process is not patterned after any step of the scientific method, but instead gives the students a chance to communicate with an audience what they have learned from their project.

For this step, the students should:

- Prepare their presentation.
- Practice their presentation.
- Share their presentation with a group of people.

Let's take a closer look at how this process works!

PREPARE THE PRESENTATION

Once the students have finished their project board, they can begin to work on their presentation. They should prepare a brief five-minute talk about their science fair project.

Here is what you need to make sure their talk includes:

- ✓ The question they tried to answer
- ✓ Their hypothesis
- ✓ A brief explanation of their experiment
- ✓ The results

✓ The conclusion to their project

You will need to guide the students as they turn their information paragraphs into an outline for their presentation. This outline should highlight the main points that they want to cover for their presentation.

Let us take a look at the outline from the sample student we have been following:

I. Question: Which soil is best for house plants to be grown in?

II. Hypothesis: If a plant is grown in a potting soil, then it will grow much faster.

III. Research:

    A. House plants grow by drawing up nutrients from the soil and using them to make energy from the sun.

    B. Vascular plants get their food from the soil, so they need it to grow.

    C. Soil is made up of rocks, minerals and decaying plants or animals.

    D. Most types of soil are a combination of these materials, which allows for variety in how the soils hold water and nutrients.

IV. Experiment:

    A. I used nine pots, grass seed, potting soil, sand, dirt from outdoors, Miracle Grow and water

    B. Explanation of the test groups (control group = soil from outside, test group #1 = potting soil, test group #2 = sand)

    C. Planted one tablespoon of grass seed in each pot and watered each of the pots with a nutrient rich solution made from Miracle Grow fertilizer and water, as needed.

    D. Set all of the pots on a window sill in full sunlight and checked the pots every day over four weeks.

    E. Recorded how much they had grown each day until the end of my experiment, once they sprouted.

V. The Results:

    A. During my experiment, I observed that all of the plants were healthy throughout the test.

    B. I noticed that the grass in test group #1 grew the best and that the grass is test group #2 grew better than the grass in the control group.

    C. Pots in test group #1 grew four and a half inches taller than the grass in test group #2

    D. Pots in test group #2 grew five inches taller than the grass in the control group.

VI. The Conclusion:

    A. I discovered that house plants grow best in potting soil, which proved my hypothesis to be true.

    B. In the future, I would like to test how water affects plant growth or how much moisture different types of soil can hold.

PRACTICE THE PRESENTATION

Once the students have finished preparing the outline for their talk, have them practice in front of a mirror. They should practice looking at the audience while pointing to the different sections on their project board as they present.

Once they feel confident with their presentation, have them give a practice talk to you. Be sure to give them feedback, so that they can make the necessary changes before they present their science fair project.

SHARE THE PRESENTATION

The ideal is to have the students present their work to an audience and answer related questions from the group. This will reinforce what they have learned as well as help them to discern how to communicate what they know.

The best way to achieve this is to have the students participate in a Science Fair where their project will be judged, but if that's not possible, don't skip this key!

The students can still present their project to their family or to a group of their peers.

You can share the following tips with your students for their presentation:

✓ Arrive on time for your presentation.

✓ Set up your project board and any other additional materials.

✓ Give your talk and then ask if there are any questions.

✓ Answer the questions and end your time by thanking whoever has come to listen to your presentation.

CONCLUSION

The keys to giving a presentation for the science fair project are to prepare, practice and share the presentation.

Once the students have shared their board and presentation with an audience, they have completed their science fair project. In the final chapter, we will share how the science fair project can look different for the high school student.

10.
THE SCIENCE FAIR PROJECT FOR THE HIGH SCHOOL STUDENT

THE HIGH SCHOOL STUDENT

1. Give them increased independence.

2. Expect in-depth scientific research.

3. Require a more complex experiment design.

Overall, high school students should show an increased depth of scientific knowledge and reasoning in regard to the science fair project.

In other words, their analysis needs to be well thought out and defended by their research and experimentation. Their conclusion should be at least several paragraphs and should include the elements previous discussed along with a discussion on how their experiment design could have effected their results. There are three key ways that you can help these students increase the difficulty of their project:

1. By giving them increased independence;
2. By expecting them to have more in-depth scientific research;
3. By requiring a more complex experiment design.

We want to clarify that the high school students we are referring to in this chapter are ones that are interested in the sciences. The students who desires to major in a science-related field, such as medicine, engineering, architecture and the sciences, should have a curriculum that includes a more in-depth science fair project, as it will prepare them for the rigors of college-level science as well as give them a strong foundation for their future careers.

The students who are not interested or struggling with science should not be expected to complete the additions to the science fair project that we are sharing about in this chapter. Instead, these students should follow the requirements laid out in the previous eight chapters or they should be allowed to opt-out of doing the science fair project altogether.

INCREASED INDEPENDENCE

Science-inclined high school students are ready to gain some independence and authority over their science fair project. Assuming that they have completed several projects throughout middle school, they have the skills and abilities in place to work self-sufficiently.

During these years, the teacher is there as an advisor. You should be there to listen to the students' ideas, to guide them towards appropriate research articles, to help them polish their experiment design and to allowing them to discuss with you their conclusions. Your goal is to help them organize their thoughts, to fuel their independent learning and to make sure that they stay on track.

These high school students should be planning, building and performing their own science fair project.

IN-DEPTH SCIENTIFIC RESEARCH

High school students are capable of more in-depth scientific research. In middle school they may have had only five references, but in high school years they will need at least fifteen to twenty references for their research. Plus,

- Their references should include scientific journals and abstracts, not just encyclopedias and non-fiction books.
- They should make use of the Internet in their research, so that they will be sure to obtain the latest information on their topic.
- Their resources need to include works published for and by scientists.

This means that they will gather a lot more information through their research.

They can still continue to use the index card method we laid out, or they can take notes on the computer using RefWorks software. In addition, their research paper will grow from one to three paragraphs to several pages. The students will also write a corresponding abstract which will give the key points of their research report to include on their project board. *See the appendix on page 55 for more information on writing an abstract.*

INCREASED COMPLEXITY OF THE EXPERIMENT DESIGN

As we alluded to in chapter five high school students will need to do multiple trials with several variables. Remember that the middle school students had only one independent variable in their project, but several controlled variables.

Now, the high school students will need to test one independent variable per trial, until they examine most, if not all, of the variables at play in the project. These additional trials will increase the complexity of their experiment design.

The students need to begin by determining the variables at work in their project. Then, they will follow the basic framework we laid out in chapter five for designing a test for each of the variables. Each of these trials will come together to form the students experiment design.

WHAT DO THESE CHANGES LOOK LIKE?

Let's examine how the high school student could have changed the project that we have been discussing to suit his abilities.

Rather than only testing which soil is best for house plants to grown in, the high school student could test whether or not traditional soil growing methods are superior to hydroponics for indoor herb plants. This project will allow the student to examine a more modern and applicable topic. It will also provide them enough variables for multiple trials that will come together to form a more complex experiment design.

The student could run three trials, one for the growth medium, one for the type of herb, and one to examine the effects of sunlight. In his first trial, he could set up two growing environments, both under grow lamps so that he can control the amount of light. This first trial would have one type of herb grown in four different mediums. One group would be grown in soil from the outdoors, one in potting soil, one in sand and finally one would be grown via hydroponics. Each of these groups would have several test plants to validate the results.

The next trial, he would have the same groups, except that now he would adjust the amount of water they receive. In the first trial he would have watered as needed, during this trial he will determine a schedule for watering the various test groups. He may need to have multiple groups in the same growth medium so that he can thoroughly examine how water affects the herbs.

Finally, once he determines which herb grows the best in the various mediums, he can test how different amounts of sunlight affect their growth. This can be done by placing several pots of each growth medium in direct sunlight, several pots in a spot that receives ambient sunlight, several pots under a grown light and several pots in the dark.

The student will still be measuring one dependent variable, the growth of the herb plant, but now he will be testing several different independent variables, such as the growth medium, the amount of water and the sunlight. Now, when he draws a conclusion about whether or not traditional growing methods are superior to hydroponics, he will have a much more accurate picture.

CONCLUSION

Although the science fair project for the science-inclined high school student seems quite challenging, you must keep in mind that they are prepared for this level of work. This will further develop their critical thinking skills and prepare them for the rigors of higher education science.

Having high school students increase the difficulty of their science fair project, by giving them increased independence, by expecting them to have more in-depth scientific research and by requiring a more complex experimental design, will give them a taste of real research and give them a leg up for their future careers.

APPENDIX

HOW TO WRITE A SCIENCE FAIR PROJECT ABSTRACT IN THREE EASY STEPS

You have worked for over a month researching, developing, and performing your science fair project.

Your board is all ready to go.

Your talk is prepared.

But as you look at the science fair requirements you read the following:

> *Your entry information should include your name and age along with the title of your project and an abstract limited to a maximum of 250 words.*

Two hundred fifty words! How in the world are you going to fit a months' worth of work into two hundred fifty words?

Relax – I'm here to share how to write a science fair abstract in three easy steps. Once you finish, you'll have a well-crafted, two-hundred-fifty-words-or-less summary of your science fair project.

STEP 1 – DEVELOP THE WORDS

To begin the process of writing an abstract for your science fair, you need to answer several questions about your project.

Here are the five key questions:

- ✓ What was your topic and why did you choose it?
- ✓ What was your hypothesis?
- ✓ What did you do for your experiment?
- ✓ What happened in your experiment?
- ✓ What did you learn from your project?

At this point, your answers need to include all the pertinent information, but still be as brief as possible.

STEP 2 – WRITE THE DRAFT

Now that you have answered the above questions, you need to write the first draft of your abstract.

Basically, you need to take your answers and add a few transitions to make it all flow into one paragraph.

As you write the draft, don't worry about the word count. You will whittle things down in the next step.

STEP 3 – WHITTLE IT DOWN

Now that you have a draft to work with, it is simply a matter of crossing out any unnecessary words until you have between one hundred and two hundred fifty words in the abstract.

Here are a few tips of things to avoid in the final draft of your abstract:

- Technical terms or abbreviations
- Direct quotes (there is no bibliography for an abstract)
- Referring to graphs or charts (again, there are no graphs or charts in your abstract)
- Things that have happened a year or more in the past
- The final abstract should be an easy-to-read, short summary of the science fair project you did.

A SAMPLE ABSTRACT

Here is an abstract from our daughter's project to give you an idea of what it can look like:

I was fascinated by an experiment we recently did on using an acid to plate copper on a nail. I wanted to explore the topic further, which why I chose to study how the pH of an acid affects copper plating. After some research, I guessed that the lower the pH the more copper would be deposited on the nail. For my experiment, I made several different solutions of acid with pH's ranging from 1 to 7. Then, I placed the pennies in each jar overnight. After that, I took out the penny and replaced it with the nail in each jar and observed what happened over three days. The nail in the solution with a pH of 1 was completely dissolved. The nail in the solution with a pH of 2 was partially dissolved. The nail in the solution with a pH of 3 had a fair amount of copper plated on it. The nail in the solution with a pH of 5 had a bit of copper. The nail in the solution with a pH of 7 was unaffected. I learned that the pH of the acid solution is important to copper plating, but unlike my hypothesis, it needs to be around pH of 3 to be the most effective.

WRAPPING IT UP

Develop your words.

Write your draft.

Whittle it down.

Follow these three easy steps and you'll have an easy-to-read summary of your science fair project.

Project by Audra W.

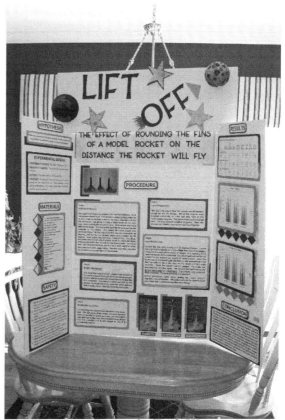

Project by Zach W.

Project by Audra W.

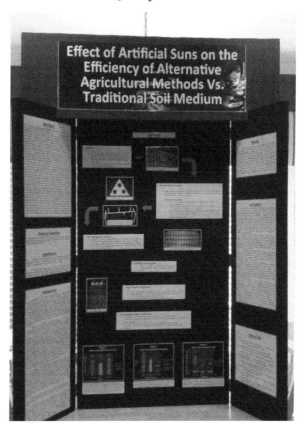

Project by Zach W.

SAMPLE SCIENCE FAIR PROJECT BOARDS

THE SCIENCE FAIR PROJECT

Student Sheets

STEP 1: CHOOSE A TOPIC

KEY 1: DECIDE ON AN AREA OF SCIENCE.

What areas of science are you interested in learning about?

_____

_____

_____

_____

_____

_____

_____

_____

_____

_____

Rank your interest in the different areas you listed and then circle the one area that you would like to use for your topic.

KEY 2: DEVELOP SEVERAL QUESTIONS ABOUT THE AREA OF SCIENCE.

What questions would you like to answer about your area of science?
Note: Remember that good questions begin with how, what, when, who, which, why, or where.

_____

_____

_____

_____

_____

_____

_____

_____

_____

_____

_____

_____

_____

KEY 3: CHOOSE A QUESTION TO BE THE TOPIC.

Write down the question that you will be using for your project.

_____

_____

_____

_____

STEP 2: DO SOME RESEARCH

KEY 1: BRAINSTORM FOR RESEARCH CATEGORIES.

What categories are you going to research for your project?

1. _____

2. _____

3. _____

4. _____

5. _____

KEY 2: RESEARCH THE CATEGORIES.

Use the following template for your research cards:

Category Number	Reference Letter
One piece of Information	

Record your sources below.

A. _____

_____

B. _____

_____

C. _____

_____

D. _____

_____

E. _____

_____

F._____

_____

G. _____

_____

H. _____

_____

I._____

_____

J. _____

_____

KEY 3: ORGANIZE THE INFORMATION.

❑ Organize the information for your report.

KEY 4: WRITE A BRIEF REPORT.

Write down what the order of your categories will be for your report.

1._____

2._____

3._____

4._____

5._____

ROUGH DRAFT

_____

_____

_____

_____

_____

_____

_____

_____

_____

_____

_____

_____

_____

_____

_____

_____

_____

_____

_____

_____

_____

_____

_____

FINAL REPORT

_____

_____

_____

_____

_____

_____

_____

_____

_____

_____

_____

_____

_____

_____

_____

_____

_____

_____

_____

_____

_____

_____

_____

_____

_____

_____

_____

STEP 2: DO SOME RESEARCH

STEP 3: FORMULATE A HYPOTHESIS

KEY 1: REVIEW THE RESEARCH.

❑ Read over your research.

KEY 2: FORMULATE AN ANSWER.

Write down your hypothesis for your science fair project.

_____

_____

_____

_____

_____

_____

STEP 4: DESIGN AN EXPERIMENT

KEY 1: CHOOSE A TEST.

What kind of a test could you use that would answer your question and prove your hypothesis either true or false?

_____

_____

_____

_____

_____

_____

_____

_____

_____

_____

_____

_____

_____

KEY 2: DETERMINE THE VARIABLES.

What is your independent variable?

_____

_____

What is your dependent variable?

_____

_____

What are your controlled variables?

_____

_____

_____

_____

KEY 3: PLAN THE EXPERIMENT.

What will the groups in your experiment be?

Control Group:_____

_____

Test Group 1:_____

_____

Test Group 2:_____

_____

Test Group 3:_____

_____

Test Group 4:_____

_____

Write down the plan for your experiment.

_____

_____

_____

_____

_____

_____

_____

KEY 4: REVIEW THE HYPOTHESIS.

❑ Verify that your experiment design will answer your hypothesis.

STEP 5: PERFORM THE EXPERIMENT

KEY 1: GET READY FOR THE EXPERIMENT.

When do you plan to run your experiment?

From_____to_____.

❑ Purchase and gather your materials.

❑ Prepare any of the materials that need to be pre-made.

KEY 2: RUN THE EXPERIMENT.

What things do you need to remember to do each day?

1. Take pictures of the experiment every day or for every trial.

2. _____

3. _____

4. _____

5. _____

6. _____

7. _____

KEY 3: RECORD ANY OBSERVATIONS AND RESULTS

OBSERVATIONS

_____

_____

_____

_____

OBSERVATIONS

_____

_____

_____

_____

_____

_____

_____

_____

_____

_____

_____

_____

_____

_____

_____

_____

_____

_____

_____

_____

_____

_____

_____

_____

_____

_____

OBSERVATIONS

_____

_____

_____

_____

_____

_____

_____

_____

_____

_____

_____

_____

_____

_____

_____

_____

_____

_____

_____

_____

_____

_____

RESULTS CHART

TIME	CONTROL GROUP	TEST GROUP 1	TEST GROUP 2	TEST GROUP 3	TEST GROUP 4

STEP 5: PERFORM THE EXPERIMENT

STEP 6: ANALYZE THE DATA

KEY 1: REVIEW AND ORGANIZE THE DATA.

What trends did you recognize in your observations?

_____

_____

_____

_____

_____

_____

_____

What information did you interpret from your results?

_____

_____

_____

_____

_____

_____

_____

_____

KEY 2: STATE THE ANSWER.

Rewrite your question (from step one):

_____

_____

_____
_____

After reviewing your data, write the answer to your question:
(Note: Your statement should begin with "I found that..." or "I discovered that...")

_____
_____
_____
_____
_____

KEY 3: DRAW SEVERAL CONCLUSIONS.

Answer the following questions:

1. Was my hypothesis proven true? (*Note: If your hypothesis was proven false, be sure to state why you think it was proven false.*)

_____
_____
_____
_____
_____

2. Did you have any problems or difficulties when performing your experiment?

_____
_____
_____
_____
_____
_____

3. Did anything interesting happen that you would like to share?

_____

_____

_____

_____

_____

_____

4. Can you think of any other things related to your project that you would like to test in the future?

_____

_____

_____

_____

_____

_____

CONCLUSION

Now take your answer from key two and your answers from key three to write you conclusion. Your paragraph should be four to six sentences in length.

_____

_____

_____

_____

_____

_____

_____

_____

_____

_____

_____

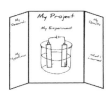

STEP 7: CREATE A BOARD

KEY 1: PLAN OUT THE BOARD.

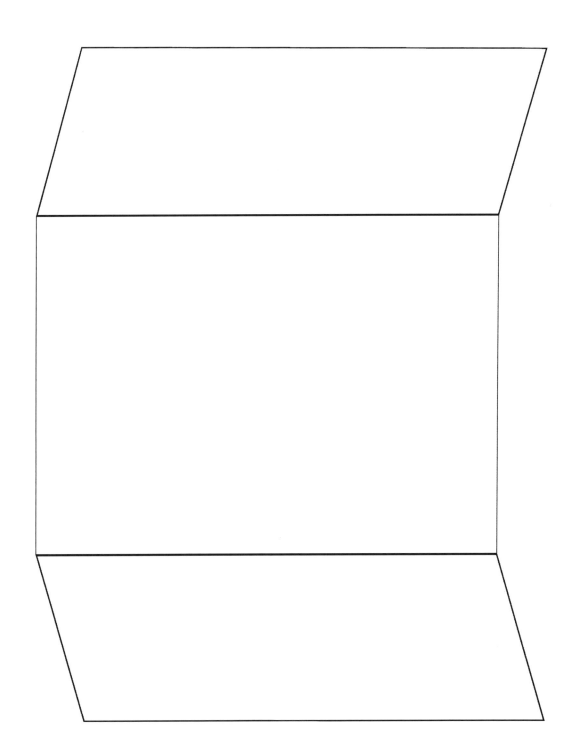

KEY 2: PREPARE THE INFORMATION.

The Introduction

Turn your question from step one into a statement. Then add two to three more sentences on why you chose your topic. Finish your paragraph by sharing the question you were trying to answer.

_____

_____

_____

_____

_____

_____

_____

_____

_____

_____

_____

_____

_____

_____

_____

❑ Type up your introduction.

The Hypothesis

❑ Type up your hypothesis from step three.

The Research

❑ Type up your research paragraph from step two.

The Materials

List your materials.

_____

_____

_____

_____

_____

❑ Type up your materials list.

The Procedure

Rewrite your experiment design in the past tense.

_____

_____

_____

_____

_____

_____

_____

_____

_____

_____

_____

_____

_____

❑ Type up your procedure.

The Results

Use your trends in the observations that you noted and the results you interpreted in step six to write a results paragraph.

_____

_____

_____

_____

_____

_____

_____

_____

_____

_____

_____

_____

_____

_____

❑ Type up results paragraph.

The Conclusion

❑ Type up your conclusion from step six.

KEY 3: PUT THE BOARD TOGETHER.

❑ Put the decorative elements on your project board.

❑ Print out and attach your information paragraphs.

❑ Add the title to your science fair project board.

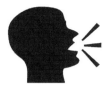

STEP 8: GIVE A PRESENTATION

KEY 1: PREPARE THE PRESENTATION.

Write down the outline for your presentation.

_____

_____

_____

_____

_____

_____

_____

_____

_____

_____

_____

_____

_____

_____

_____

_____

_____

_____

_____

_____

_____

_____

_____

_____

_____

_____

_____

_____

_____

_____

_____

_____

_____

_____

_____

_____

_____

KEY 2: PRACTICE THE PRESENTATION.

❏ Practice your presentation in front of a mirror several times.

❏ Practice your presentation with your teacher.

KEY 3: SHARE THE PRESENTATION.

Keep the following tips in mind for your presentation:

❏ Arrive on time for your presentation.

❏ Set up your project board and any other additional materials.

❏ Give your talk and then ask if there are any questions.

❏ Answer the questions and end your time by thanking whomever has come to listen to your presentation.